Orton Gillingham
Red Words

Orton Gillingham activities and resources to help
children read and write

VOLUME 3

Adriana Robertson

INTRODUCTION

Dyslexia is a neurodevelopmental disorder that manifests itself in those who have difficulties learning to read through conventional means and techniques. Dyslexia can be described as a learning disability that appears during the early stages of development and presents differently as the person grows older. These problems tend to appear during childhood and can persist throughout the person's adolescence and even adulthood.

Why Phonological Awareness Is Effective

In the same way that, in order to learn how to do number operations we must first understand that a number is the graphic representation of a value, when learning to read, certain skill sets need to be acquired before starting to read. Not all children develop these skills equally; many times they begin learning to read without being prepared for it.

Training phonological awareness allows the student to understand the segmental structure of language and develop their abilities to discriminate, categorize, associate and synthesize linguistic information.

How to develop a phonological awareness program

Phonological awareness must be instructed in order to be effective, so the first thing when treating a child with dyslexia is to conduct a good evaluation. Once evaluated in level, we will know what the child's greatest difficulties are when it comes to writing and reading.

Red Word Practice **on**

Read it.

on

Color it.

on

Write it.

_____

_____

_____

Clap it.

How many syllables?

1   2   3

Circle the vowels.

on

How many vowels did you find?

....

Connect the letters.

f   p   s   k

u   o   n   t

Write a sentence using the sight word.

_____

_____

Red Word Practice **at**

Read it.

at

Color it.

at

Write it.

Clap it.

How many syllables?

1 2 3

Circle the vowels.

at

How many vowels did you find?

....

Connect the letters.

h a e l

v c b t

Write a sentence using the sight word.

Red Word Practice **must**

Read it.

must

Color it.

must

Write it.

Clap it.

How many syllables?

1   2   3

Circle the vowels.

must

How many vowels did you find?

Connect the letters.

m   j   s   z

u   n   a   t

Write a sentence using the sight word.

Red Word Practice   into

Read it	Color it
into	into

Write it

_____

_____

Clap it

How many syllables?

1   2   3

Circle the vowels

into

How many vowels did you find?

⬭

Connect the letters

l   i   a   g

b   n   t   o

Write a sentence using the sight word

_____

_____

Red Word Practice **no**

Read it.

no

Color it.

no

Write it.

Clap it.

How many syllables?

1   2   3

Circle the vowels.

no

How many vowels did you find?

Connect the letters.

d p n h

w o m t

Write a sentence using the sight word.

Red Word Practice **do**

Read it.

do

Color it.

do

Write it.

Clap it.

How many syllables?

1   2   3

Circle the vowels.

do

How many vowels did you find?

⬯

Connect the letters.

d   p   a   j

z   o   e   v

Write a sentence using the sight word.

Red Word Practice **have**

Read it.

have

Color it.

have

Write it.

_____
_____
_____

Clap it.

How many syllables?

1 2 3

Circle the vowels.

have

How many vowels did you find?

◯ ....

Connect the letters.

h p v r

z a n e

Write a sentence using the sight word.

_____
_____

Read it.

but

Color it.

but

Write it.

Clap it.

How many syllables?

1 2 3

Circle the vowels.

but

How many vowels did you find?

Connect the letters.

q b u h

a o i t

Write a sentence using the sight word.

Red Word Practice **well**

Read it.

well

Color it.

well

Write it.

Clap it.

How many syllables?

1 2 3

Circle the vowels.

well

How many vowels did you find?

Connect the letters.

f g e b

w o l l

Write a sentence using the sight word.

Red Word Practice too

Read it.

too

Color it.

too

Write it.

Clap it.

How many syllables?

1 2 3

Circle the vowels.

too

How many vowels did you find?

⬭

Connect the letters.

t   p   o   q

z   o   n   f

Write a sentence using the sight word.

Read it.

ran

Color it.

ran

Write it.

_____

_____

_____

_____

Clap it.

How many syllables?

1   2   3

Circle the vowels.

ran

How many vowels did you find?

⬭ ....

Connect the letters.

h   p   r   u

z   a   n   t

Write a sentence using the sight word.

_____

_____

Red Word Practice **new**

Read it.

new

Color it.

new

Write it.

_____

Clap it.

How many syllables?

1 2 3

Circle the vowels.

new

How many vowels did you find?

Connect the letters.

a p e k

u q n w

Write a sentence using the sight word.

Red Word Practice that

Read it.

that

Color it.

that

Write it.

_____

Clap it.

How many syllables?

1 2 3

Circle the vowels.

that

How many vowels did you find?

_____

Connect the letters.

t h s k

u o a t

Write a sentence using the sight word.

_____

Red Word Practice **all**

Read it.

all

Color it.

all

Write it.

_____

Clap it.

How many syllables?

1 2 3

Circle the vowels.

all

How many vowels did you find?

....

Connect the letters.

d m a l
u o l t

Write a sentence using the sight word.

_____

Red Word Practice **SO**

Read it.

SO

Color it.

SO

Write it.

_____

_____

_____

_____

Clap it.

How many syllables?

1   2   3

Circle the vowels.

SO

How many vowels did you find?

⬭ ....

Connect the letters.

f   p   s   k

u   o   n   t

Write a sentence using the sight word.

_____

_____

Red Word Practice   four

Read it.

four

Color it.

four

Write it.

Clap it.

How many syllables?

1   2   3

Circle the vowels.

four

How many vowels did you find?

Connect the letters.

w   f   u   k

c   o   r   t

Write a sentence using the sight word.

Red Word Practice   **they**

Read it.

they

Color it.

they

Write it.

_____

_____

_____

Clap it.

How many syllables?

1   2   3

Circle the vowels.

they

How many vowels did you find?

Connect the letters.

t   h   s   y

u   o   e   p

Write a sentence using the sight word.

_____

Red Word Practice   like

Read it
like

Color it
like

Write it

Clap it
How many syllables?

1 2 3

Circle the vowels
like

How many vowels did you find?

_____

Connect the letters

l p s k

i o e t

Write a sentence using the sight word

Red Word Practice there

Read it.

there

Color it.

there

Write it.

_____

_____

_____

Clap it.

How many syllables?

1   2   3

Circle the vowels.

there

How many vowels did you find?

(..........)

Connect the letters.

j   t   h   f

e   r   e   w

Write a sentence using the sight word.

_____

_____

Red Word Practice **he**

Read it.
he

Color it.
he

Write it.

Clap it.
How many syllables?

1   2   3

Circle the vowels.
he

How many vowels did you find?

Connect the letters.

h   g   s   k

u   e   m   t

Write a sentence using the sight word.

Read it.

be

Color it.

be

Write it.

Clap it.

How many syllables?

1 2 3

Circle the vowels.

be

How many vowels did you find?

Connect the letters.

j   q   s   b

u   o   e   t

Write a sentence using the sight word.

Red Word Practice **am**

Read it.

am

Color it.

am

Write it.

Clap it.

How many syllables?

1   2   3

Circle the vowels.

am

How many vowels did you find?

....

Connect the letters.

b   k   s   h

u   a   m   t

Write a sentence using the sight word.

Read it.

soon

Color it.

soon

Write it.

_____

_____

_____

Clap it.

How many syllables?

(1) (2) (3)

Circle the vowels.

soon

How many vowels did you find?

(..........)

Connect the letters.

f   p   s   o

u   o   n   t

Write a sentence using the sight word.

_____

_____

Read it.

now

Color it.

now

Write it.

_____

_____

_____

Clap it.

How many syllables?

1 2 3

Circle the vowels.

now

How many vowels did you find?

(..........)

Connect the letters.

b l o q

w e n x

Write a sentence using the sight word.

_____

_____

Red Word Practice **are**

Read it.

are

Color it.

are

Write it.

_____

_____

Clap it.

How many syllables?

1   2   3

Circle the vowels.

are

How many vowels did you find?

(.........)

Connect the letters.

f   p   a   k

u   r   n   e

Write a sentence using the sight word.

_____

_____

Read it.

did

Color it.

did

Write it.

Clap it.

How many syllables?

1 2 3

Circle the vowels.

did

How many vowels did you find?

Connect the letters.

d w d z

c i q n

Write a sentence using the sight word.

Red Word Practice ate

Read it.

ate

Color it.

ate

Write it.

Clap it.

How many syllables?

1
2
3

Circle the vowels.

ate

How many vowels did you find?

⟨........⟩

Connect the letters.

a t s k
e z v h

Write a sentence using the sight word.

Red Word Practice get

Read it.
get

Color it.
get

Write it.

Clap it.
How many syllables?

1 2 3

Circle the vowels.
get

How many vowels did you find?

Connect the letters.

g p e k

v z n t

Write a sentence using the sight word.

Red Word Practice   **out**

Read it.

out

Color it.

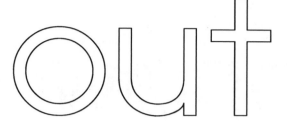

Write it.

_____

_____

_____

Clap it.

How many syllables?

Circle the vowels.

out

How many vowels did you find?

Connect the letters.

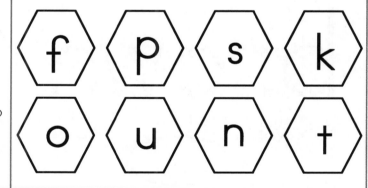

Write a sentence using the sight word.

_____

_____

Read it.

brown

Color it.

brown

Write it.

_____

- - - - - - - - - - - - - - - - - - - -

_____

_____

Clap it.

How many syllables?

(1) (2) (3)

Circle the vowels.

brown

How many vowels did you find?

(.........)

Connect the letters.

(b) (p) (w) (k)

(r) (o) (n) (t)

Write a sentence using the sight word.

_____

- -

Red Word Practice **eat**

Read it.

eat

Color it.

eat

Write it.

Clap it.

How many syllables?

1
2
3

Circle the vowels.

eat

How many vowels did you find?

Connect the letters.

k   q   e   l

a   c   w   t

Write a sentence using the sight word.

Read it.

our

Color it.

our

Write it.

Clap it.

How many syllables?

1 2 3

Circle the vowels.

our

How many vowels did you find?

Connect the letters.

o b r h

u i n t

Write a sentence using the sight word.

Red Word Practice **saw**

Read it.

saw

Color it.

saw

Write it.

Clap it.

How many syllables?

1 2 3

Circle the vowels.

saw

How many vowels did you find?

Connect the letters.

q h s f

v a w k

Write a sentence using the sight word.

Red Word Practice say

Read it.

say

Color it.

say

Write it.

Clap it.

How many syllables?

1 2 3

Circle the vowels.

say

How many vowels did you find?

Connect the letters.

z p s a

u o y h

Write a sentence using the sight word.

Red Word Practice ride

Read it.
ride

Color it.
ride

Write it.

_____

_____

_____

Clap it.
How many syllables?

1 2 3

Circle the vowels.
ride

How many vowels did you find?

_____

Connect the letters.
i d c k

r a e t

Write a sentence using the sight word.

_____

_____

Red Word Practice **pretty**

Read it.

pretty

Color it.

pretty

Write it.

_____

Clap it.

How many syllables?

1 2 3

Circle the vowels.

pretty

How many vowels did you find?

(............)

Connect the letters.

f   p   t   y

r   e   n   t

Write a sentence using the sight word.

_____

_____

Read it.

she

Color it.

she

Write it.

_____

_____

_____

Clap it.

How many syllables?

(1) (2) (3)

Circle the vowels.

she

How many vowels did you find?

(..........)

Connect the letters.

b   p   s   m

u   h   e   t

Write a sentence using the sight word.

_____

_____

Red Word Practice   black

Read it.

black

Color it.

black

Write it.

Clap it.

How many syllables?

1   2   3

Circle the vowels.

black

How many vowels did you find?

Connect the letters.

b   p   a   k

u   l   c   t

Write a sentence using the sight word.

Read it.

good

Color it.

good

Write it.

_____

_____

_____

Clap it.

How many syllables?

1   2   3

Circle the vowels.

good

How many vowels did you find?

_____

Connect the letters.

g   p   s   d

u   o   o   t

Write a sentence using the sight word.

_____

_____

Red Word Practice come

Read it.

came

Color it.

came

Write it.

Clap it.

How many syllables?

1 2 3

Circle the vowels.

came

How many vowels did you find?

....

Connect the letters.

h a e b

c o m g

Write a sentence using the sight word.

Red Word Practice   **on**

Look for the sight word | **on** | and color all of them.

but	on	this	he
on	he		so
on	saw	on	ride
out		was	on
on	on	pretty	all

Cut and paste to spell the sight word.

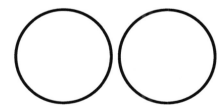

Red Word Practice **at**

Look for the sight word [**at**] and color all of them.

came	at	at	he
	pretty	ride	have
on	at	soon	at
	black	at	be
four	eat	at	at

Cut and paste to spell the sight word.

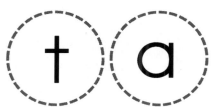

Red Word Practice **must**

Look for the sight word | must | and color all of them.

must   well   be   they

do   must   must

did   say   must   please

at   on   came

must   eat   must   must

Cut and paste to spell the sight word.

◯ ◯ ◯ ◯

t   u   m   s

Red Word Practice **into**

Look for the sight word | into | and color all of them.

into	under	yes	into
into		went	came
do	into	must	on
into		at	eat
have	good	into	into

Cut and paste to spell the sight word.

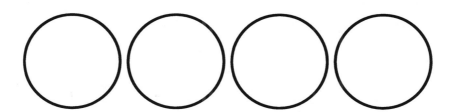

t i o n

Red Word Practice **no**

Look for the sight word [**no**] and color all of them.

no	pretty	good	they
ride	do		no
on	at	no	be
soon	black	no	
came	no	four	no

Cut and paste to spell the sight word.

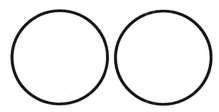

Red Word Practice   do

Look for the sight word | do | and color all of them.

do   ate   do   but

get   four   do

do   ate   all   too

no   soon   do

black   do   so   will

Cut and paste to spell the sight word.

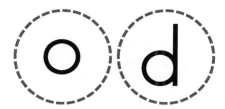

Red Word Practice have

Look for the sight word  and color all of them.

have	into	have	do
soon	like	went
do	have	new	have
but	brown	have
have	are	he	have

Cut and paste to spell the sight word.

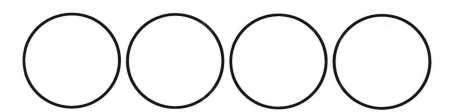

Red Word Practice **but**

Look for the sight word  and color all of them.

but	yes	will	but
like		are	soon
but	do	did	but
went		have	brown
but	but	there	out

Cut and paste to spell the sight word.

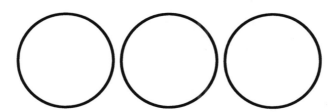

Red Word Practice **well**

Look for the sight word and color all of them.

well	that	like	well
into	well		soon
he	well	must	now
all	well		ate
good	have	black	well

Cut and paste to spell the sight word.

Red Word Practice **too**

Look for the sight word | **too** | and color all of them.

saw	please	too	too
	ran	went	brown
too	too	she	too
	soon	black	came
too	who	too	will

Cut and paste to spell the sight word.

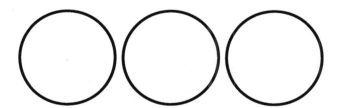

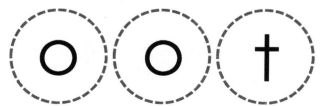

Red Word Practice **ran**

Look for the sight word | ran | and color all of them.

too	ran	saw	do
	ran	came	ran
she	he	ran	ran
	soon	who	brown
will	ran	ran	came

Cut and paste to spell the sight word.

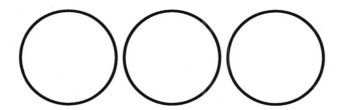

Red Word Practice **new**

Look for the sight word | **new** | and color all of them.

will   new   new   ran

who   new   came

he   too   who   new

    new   get   new

be   now   brown   under

Cut and paste to spell the sight word.

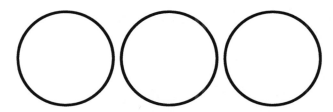

e   w   n

Red Word Practice   **that**

Look for the sight word  and color all of them.

that	that	who	out
do	that	did	
will	there	she	that
that	came	that	
this	that	that	good

Cut and paste to spell the sight word.

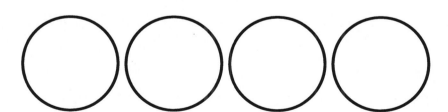

h   t   a   t

Red Word Practice **all**

Look for the sight word | all | and color all of them.

all   but   all   all

yes   went   out

have   all   all   did

there   who   like

all   four   be   all

Cut and paste to spell the sight word.

◯ ◯ ◯

l   a   l

Red Word Practice **SO**

Look for the sight word [**so**] and color all of them.

now	so	want	she
what	so		so
do	will	black	so
yes	so		did
on	so	so	pretty

Cut and paste to spell the sight word.

Red Word Practice **four**

Look for the sight word | four | and color all of them.

four   soon   four   too

like   four   have

did   four   are   all

four   four   brown

four   ate   pretty   four

Cut and paste to spell the sight word.

u   r   f   o

Red Word Practice **they**

Look for the sight word **they** and color all of them.

they	that	will	did
soon	they	they
get	they	came	too
they	black	they
eat	all	they	good

Cut and paste to spell the sight word.

 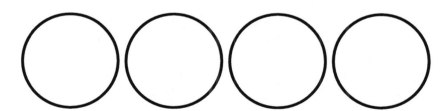

 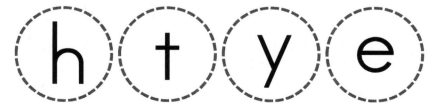

Red Word Practice like

Look for the sight word and color all of them.

like	there	like	too
they		like	like
all	ate	like	like
will	who	ride
like	ran	good	do

Cut and paste to spell the sight word.

i   k   l   e

Red Word Practice **there**

Look for the sight word | **there** | and color all of them.

there	that	there	get
soon		there	did
he	there	must	there
now	have		good
there	there	black	well

Cut and paste to spell the sight word.

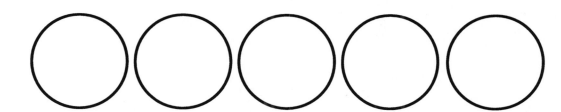

e h r t e

Red Word Practice he

Look for the sight word | **he** | and color all of them.

came	he	he	he
	pretty	ride	have
do	he	soon	he
	black	he	be
he	eat	four	he

Cut and paste to spell the sight word.

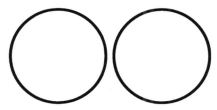

Red Word Practice be

Look for the sight word | **be** | and color all of them.

be	ate	do	will
get	four		be
be	be	all	too
no	soon		be
brown	be	yes	be

Cut and paste to spell the sight word.

- -

Red Word Practice **am**

Look for the sight word [**am**] and color all of them.

but	am	this	am
on		he	am
am	saw	am	ride
out	was		am
will	am	ate	am

Cut and paste to spell the sight word.

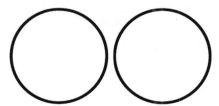

Red Word Practice **soon**

Look for the sight word | **soon** | and color all of them.

soon	under	yes	into
will	went	came
do	soon	must	soon
soon	soon	eat
have	good	soon	eat

Cut and paste to spell the sight word.

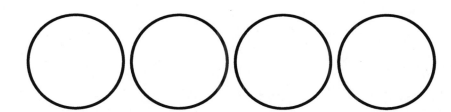

Red Word Practice **now**

Look for the sight word [**now**] and color all of them.

but	yes	will	now
like	now		soon
now	do	now	did
went	now	brown	
now	with	now	now

Cut and paste to spell the sight word.

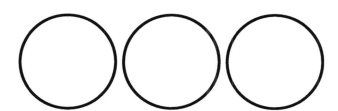

- -

o w n

Red Word Practice **are**

Look for the sight word [**are**] and color all of them.

saw	please	are	are
are	will		black
went	are	she	are
are	black	all	
are	came	are	are

Cut and paste to spell the sight word.

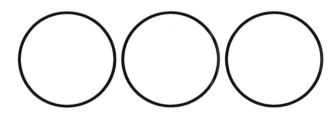

- -

r   a   e

Red Word Practice **did**

Look for the sight word | **did** | and color all of them.

did   under   yes   did

    into   did   came

there   did   must   did

    did   at   eat

have   good   did   they

Cut and paste to spell the sight word.

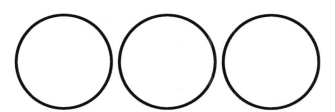

Red Word Practice **ate**

Look for the sight word [ate] and color all of them.

eat	ate	ate	ran
who		ate	ate
he	too	who	ate
ate	get	will	
be	ate	brown	under

Cut and paste to spell the sight word.

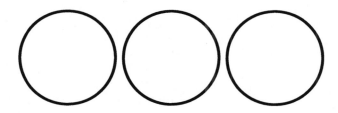

t e a

Red Word Practice **get**

Look for the sight word | get | and color all of them.

get   ran   saw   get

will   came   get

she   he   with   get

soon   who   brown

get   ran   get   get

Cut and paste to spell the sight word.

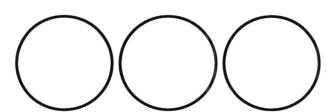

t   g   e

Red Word Practice **out**

Look for the sight word **out** and color all of them.

out	will	out	all
	with	went	out
yes	out	out	did
	there	have	like
out	four	be	out

Cut and paste to spell the sight word.

 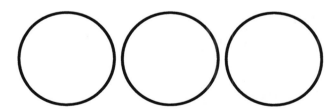

u t o

Red Word Practice **brown**

Look for the sight word  and color all of them.

brown	into	brown	did
	will	like	went
with	brown	new	brown
	but	brown	have
brown	please	she	brown

Cut and paste to spell the sight word.

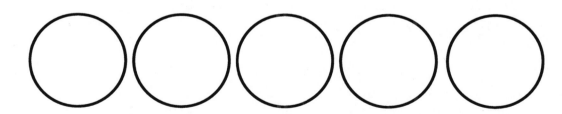

Red Word Practice **eat**

Look for the sight word and color all of them.

do	eat	eat	with
black	four		four
eat	ate	good	be
eat	did		eat
brown	must	eat	there

 Cut and paste to spell the sight word.

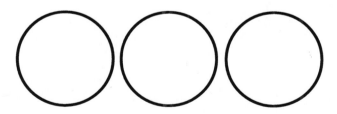

Red Word Practice **our**

Look for the sight word [**our**] and color all of them.

out	that	like	our
	into	our	soon
now	our	must	our
	will	our	eat
our	our	ate	yes

Cut and paste to spell the sight word.

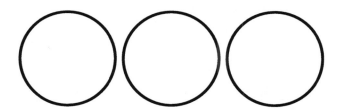

Red Word Practice **saw**

Look for the sight word [**saw**] and color all of them.

saw	ran	saw	do
with	came		saw
she	he	black	saw
soon	saw	brown	
will	saw	saw	did

Cut and paste to spell the sight word.

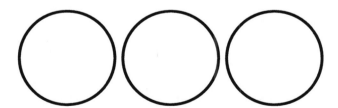

Red Word Practice **say**

Look for the sight word | **say** | and color all of them.

say   yes   will   say

like   say   soon

are   do   did   say

have   say   brown

say   say   they   say

Cut and paste to spell the sight word.

○ ○ ○

Red Word Practice **ride**

Look for the sight word | ride | and color all of them.

ride	that	like	ride
she		ride	soon
he	ride	must	ride
all	ride		ate
ride	have	black	will

Cut and paste to spell the sight word.

i   d   e   r

Red Word Practice **pretty**

Look for the sight word | pretty | and color all of them.

will	pretty	new	ran
	with	pretty	have
he	too	pretty	do
pretty	get		pretty
be	now	pretty	under

Cut and paste to spell the sight word.

○ ○ ○ ○ ○ ○

 r p t e y t

Red Word Practice   **she**

Look for the sight word   **she**   and color all of them.

she	soon	she	too
	with	she	have
did	four	are	all
	she	she	please
will	ate	pretty	she

Cut and paste to spell the sight word.

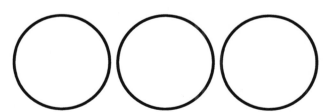

Red Word Practice **black**

Look for the sight word  and color all of them.

black	there	will	our
please	black	too	
will	there	she	black
that	came	black	
have	black	black	good

Cut and paste to spell the sight word.

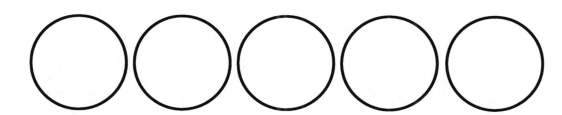

Red Word Practice good

Look for the sight word good and color all of them.

with	good	yes	into
	will	went	came
do	good	must	good
	good	soon	eat
she	good	good	eat

Cut and paste to spell the sight word.

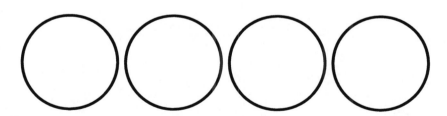

o d o g

Red Word Practice **came**

Look for the sight word | came | and color all of them.

came   that   like   our

into   came   soon

now   came   must   came

will   came   eat

pretty   came   ate   yes

Cut and paste to spell the sight word.

a   m   e   c

Made in the USA
Las Vegas, NV
27 November 2024

12778142R00070